1-91

Matt + Julie,
Congratulations + much happiness!

Denise + Bob

D1094596

to our soulmates

Harrison, Marvel • Kellogg, Terry • Michaels, Greg

ISBN 1-56073-00201

Printed in the United States of America

Other Books Offered By BRAT Publishing:

Broken Toys Broken Dreams *Understanding and Healing Codependency, Compulsive Behaviors and Family:* Terry Kellogg

AttrACTIVE WOMEN *A Physical Fitness Approach To Emotional & Spiritual Well-Being:* Marvel Harrison & Catharine Stewart-Roache

Butterfly Kisses *Little Intimacies For Sharing!* Harrison & Kellogg & Michaels

Hummingbird Words *Self Affirmations & Notes To Nurture By:* Harrison & Kellogg & Michaels

Roots & Wings *Words For Growing A Family:* Harrison & Kellogg & Michaels

BRAT Publishing, Suite 225, 6 University Drive, Amherst, MA 01002
1-800-359-BRAT (2728)

butterfly kisses
little intimacies that can't be bought, sometimes noticed, sometimes not

marvel harrison   terry kellogg

illustrations by greg michaels

BRAT PUBLISHING

*h*ave you ever been very close to someone special and felt the wisp of an eyelash brush your cheek? you have been touched by the flutter of a butterfly kiss.

*b*utterfly kisses are gifts given and gifts received that build and maintain intimacy. some may not feel like gifts, a few might be scary, all involve taking risks. butterfly kisses are the precious moments in life we share and cherish with roommates, soulmates and playmates.

a book for anyone who hasn't given up completely and even they might secretly enjoy it!

*n*otice—especially little things

affirm all you can

cherish differences

let what is given be enough

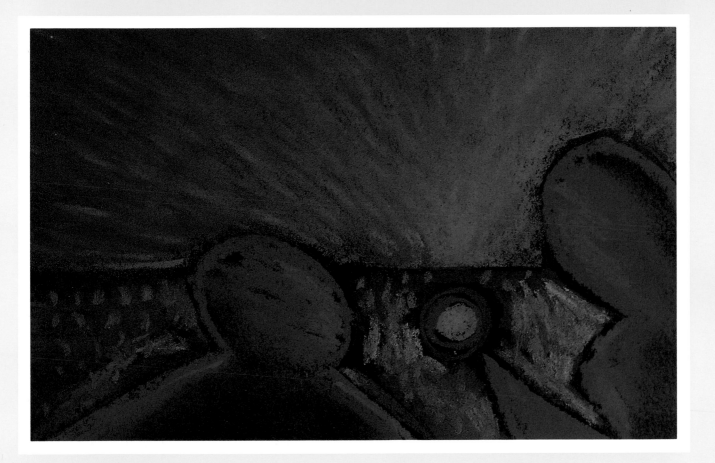

*d*ance alone

dance together

cherish childness

hold hands

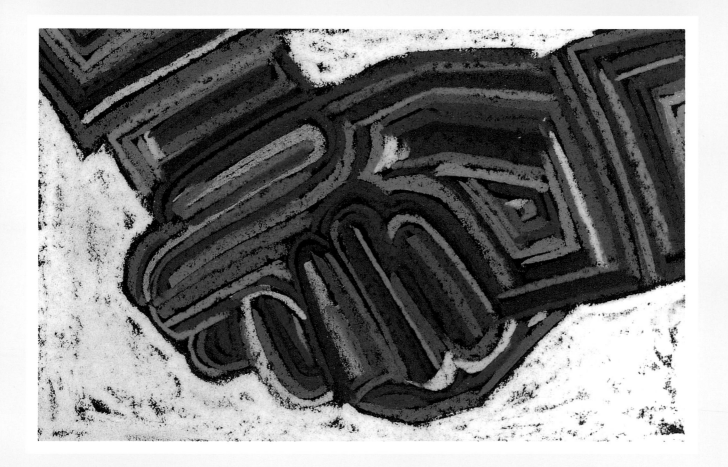

*t*alk even when it is difficult

write what you can't say

send flowers

do lunch

chat

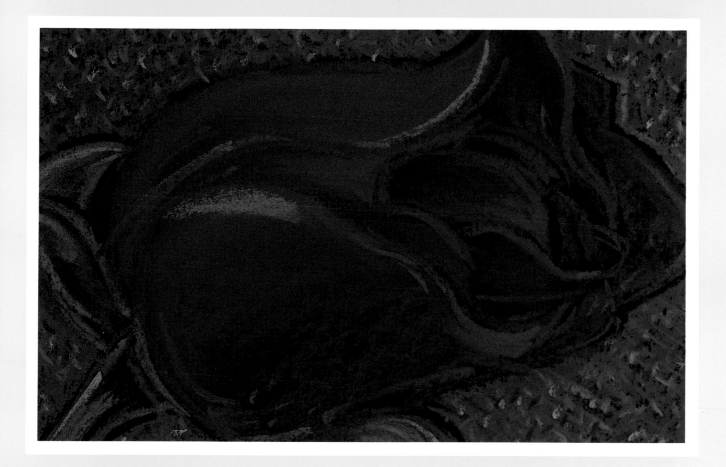

*k*now yourself

tell stories

record your history

laugh, play and work

whisper, wink and giggle

snuggle

embrace your inner brat

*g*o slow, intimacy builds with time

be vulnerable

touch tears

grieve

*d*on't compete

don't be cheap

don't be a creep

*g*ive up perfection

learn to fight

respect boundaries and privacy

allow silence

*S*hare beliefs and goals

walk in their shoes

sacrifice

support a cause

*t*ake a risk

make choices and mistakes

stay connected

forgive

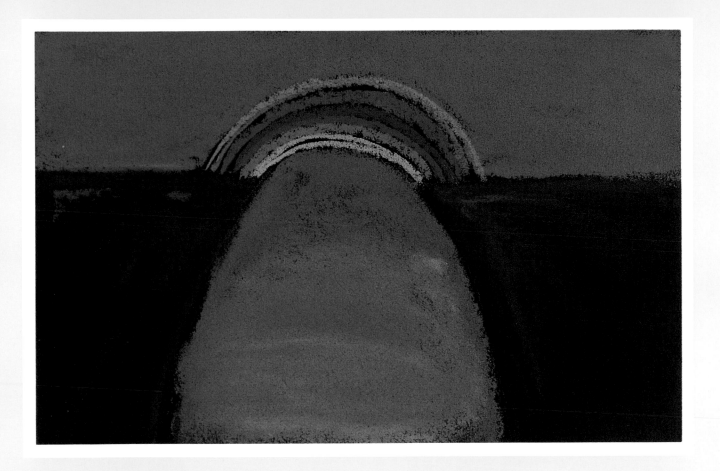

*r*emember real crises are rare

solve the problems you can

let some problems resolve themselves

let some problems remain problems

*b*end don't break

give up control

accept reality

break bread

make music

share candlelight

grow something

*t*ouch

talk about pleasuring

take time outs

*i*nvest in self

enhance talents

look for joy within

network

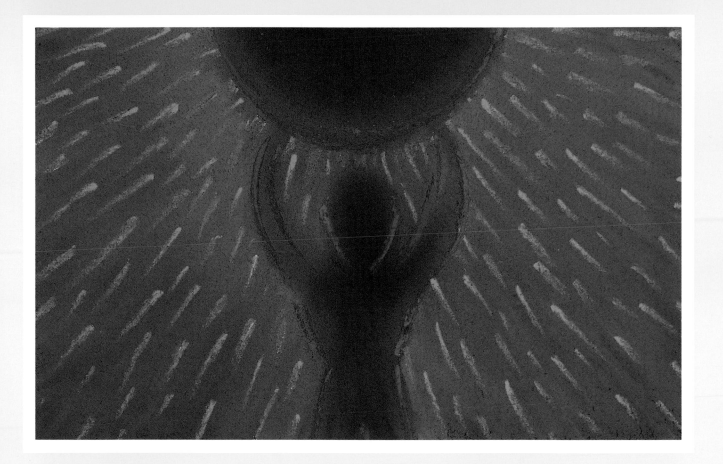

*r*elish your body

share physical challenges

accept each other's pace

*C*omment gently
offer alternatives
show respect

*C*reate celebrations

ride ferris wheels, carousels and

roller coasters

believe in your magic

let your spirit soar

*r*espect rituals

notice creation

share gratitude

join in a spiritual journey

*a*nticipate rapids, waves

and still water

learn prayer and humor as postures

towards life and each other

Marvel Harrison, a native of Canada, is an avid runner, skier, canoeist and and likes to play. She is a PhD candidate in Counseling Psychology, author, therapist and lecturer specializing in a gentle approach to self acceptance. Marvel's spirit and zest for life are easily felt by audiences everywhere.

Terry Kellogg is a parent, athlete, counselor and teacher. For twenty years he has been helping families with compulsive and addictive behaviors. Besides writing poetry, he is a wilderness enthusiast and advocate for vulnerable groups and our planet. Terry is an entertaining, challenging, inspiring and much sought after speaker.

Gregory Michaels is a full time Dad and a free lance graphic designer. His clever wit and sensitivity to children of all ages are apparent in his work and he has a terrific sense of humor to boot! Greg and his family make their home in the Rocky Mountains of Colorado.